a date with Rain

a date with Rain

what happens to a raindrop once it meets the ocean?

Jennifer Agostini

Published by Tablo

Table of Contents

acknowledgments

To you, the reader, thank you for believing in me.
To me, the writer, thank you for believing in me.
To us, the beings, thank you for believing in the power of connection.
To all who have ever wished to experience unity with nature, thank you
for giving this a chance to take you there.
To the Flo of life, thank you for embarking on the journey to deeply relate
to this prose.

a sometimes-perfect date

he is highly honeyed
and murmurs melodiously
brushing his gentle touch
across each edge of my skin, melting
into all parts of my body, already
unclothed

his tender strokes reach
all along and across me
plating shivers for dinner
deeply dripping down my spine
making the hairs on my body stand tall
covering the shape of my frame
gratifying goosebumps
for the very first time

he creates congenial music for me
the beat seldomly fast
moments where the tempo has slowed
unblemished and imperfect

although,
while we are stuck together
we always dance together

sometimes he will join me
when he isn't desired
the sight is unfortunate
making it dangerous
for him to be prancing
around me

he can be such an infliction of pain
yet, I love him so dearly
because no matter what
he's always earnestly nurturing me

he's the finest and wickedest date
yet, always the most memorable

and so, if you'd let me
I'd like to introduce you
to my date with Rain

leap to freedom

is she too nervous, to take
the vast leap off the cliff of the sky
into this unknown below
like so many of us can be

at least we can empathize with her
it takes commitment to live up to a vow
once you do start falling
you're never gonna stop, until you land

find peace in space of that body,
of soft and salty champagne
that which we all often see, pondering
that cosmic outlandish slice of this planet

and can you believe,
she actually has *hesitancy*
to drop?
can't you see?

that's us, too nervous
to take the leap of trust

a plunge into devotion
a hop into freedom

of and within ourselves, simultaneously
transforming lives

it's only because we don't know
the most beautiful part of the story
is waiting at the bottom
to catch us free fallin'

scent

it's pouring
dime-sized drops of rain
earth is washing herself off
laying on a layer of perfume
freshly across her chest
like it's her first date
with the sun
again

hold me

wind blows
drops land
trees call
leaves dance
fog rolls in

I'm surrounded
and feel all alone
until everything encasing me disappears

it's then that the Earth steps in
and holds me
with such relaxed ease

veda

a drop of rain
is a message from the sky
reminding us that it's a simple sole
in the wild whole ocean

witness that when all these droplets come together
it feeds and connects the full world

like fine wine

stepping out of my home
feet dropping onto the first step, nearly
slipping as the rain begins crashing, falling
down in thick translucent sheets
blurring the whole world around me

I want to last in this weather forever
every time I believe I won't come back
the sheets mask my sight

I can take the risk
but, I want a drive
without a fight

I could hate and thrash and cry
pouting back at home
I could dance and sing and love and moan
drinking every single sip of heavy rain and wine

with glorious greed
of that sky-fallen shower
we're gifted with each end of November

my pores drink
like a sommelier
inviting in that first delicious drop
swashing it all around the mouth
squeezing cheeks as the tannins become full and ripe

nourishment flushes through me
better than the everyday downpour
in my musky dewy bathroom

but this,
was just like that inconceivably fine plum drink
the one we had the night we got married
cheap, sweet, and serving us
with boundless love

if this was just the wine
and it wasn't even at its finest,
I'm looking forward to you
serving me the whole delectable feast

waiting

I sit quietly, each time
the rain starts falling, I close my eyes
and feel the rush of the wind
and the sprinkle of dew
like a soft mist

waiting for answers
from our Mother, herself
her wisdom starts sinking
deep into me

do you ever sit and wait?
just to see what happens
when answers come to you
instead of always chasing after them?

because nothing ever comes
until I close my eyes
and the rain starts falling
each time, only when
I sit quietly,
waiting

first fall

moments after the pouring rain
the scent of petrichor blows up my nose
it's better than whiffs of cocaine
eternally teasing me to forget

this time it's worth the high
eradicating the comedown from drowning me
encouraging me to remember
who I am

weight

leaves losing weight
rain making its way to the ground

enriching the roots
through the abundant soil

sustenance of the water begins
to rush its way back up

the delicious tantalizing trunk
giving strength to the foliage
to hold more

and lead to a free flowing river
that forever feeds
all the breathing beautiful Beings

accompanied

do you remember that one time it rained
and you felt sad and anguished for the world?

do you remember that one time it rained
and you wanted to cry in agony with the sky?

do you remember that one time it rained
and you healed heroically after your worst romantic disband?

do you remember that one time it rained
and you buried yourself in the covers to disguise?

do you remember that one time it rained
and you drank so much coffee that your skin ran dry?

do you remember that one time it rained
and you were desolated of the unwelcomed forlorn?

do you remember that one time it rained?
I have a secret for you:
you were not alone.

raise

reminisce to your recapture by the rain
you danced because it's all you could do
you lavished in a creative stream
you stretched your emotions
as you played author all evening

reminisce to your recapture by the rain
you coupled so deeply
you wailed affinity into the night
you experienced mastery
as you caressed and kissed everlastingly

reminisce to your recapture by the rain
you played with your tribe
you embraced under the wash
your candid hunger erupted
as you danced with the stream

reminisce to your recapture by the rain
thank her
be grateful for her
she raised you

take off your shoes

soak your feet,
in the mucky ground

close your eyes,
look up to the sky

and stay,
keep waiting
until the rain starts falling

and watch,
as you are washed

endowed a clean slate, creating
for you, a new beginning

vocation

a pulsating fall
dripping grimly on the treehouse
precipitates firing down from the sky
a warning of the storm coming in stronger
earth waving her arms and shaking the ground
shifting with speed and holding on for dear life
moving like an invitation, calling us to lean
in mischievously and head her message

now, just take a moment to notice
just how much they surrender
so loyal to who they are
and their divine
intention

wise people,
with meaning
they are all here
swallowing ignorance
redeeming godlike significance

uninvited

dropping himself off at our feet
already overstayed
yet irrevocably loved

welcoming himself into our living room
every Saturday afternoon
breaking plans for an evening out
spending hours in the bath
regardless of our guidance
asking him to go

and he welcomes himself in
and we're underprepared, yet satisfied
about to marinate in the delicious juices of relating
and correlating
our bodies
as they come together

a connection we wouldn't usually get
if this friend *actually* respected boundaries
often arriving
as an interruption
we want to turn away at the door

we don't, because
we know just how nourishing it is
for us to allow
this uninvited guest
to drop himself off
and empty his emotions
all over our floor

waves

once I was given an opportunity
to lie down
and scream

so, I could watch all the waves of confusion
wash over me
and I just sat, waiting

for days for the wash to come out clean
I wanted my laundry to do itself
as I rested abidingly

convincing me to rest uselessly
but nothing ever came
until I lied down once again

and screamed for the last time
as the swell of bewilderment
finished washing over me

it was then that I realized
I had no despairs or reservations
the wash had already come out clean

charm

impatience as I cry up to the sky
a testament to what awakens beneath me

ceasing the need of conjuring up thoughts
leaving it all up to time and wisdom

waiting eagerly for it to release
metamorphosing from dirty wash to pristine

like an autumn leaf at the top of a tree
running the splash, becoming clean

it wasn't until I took the time, to listen
patiently, sensually spoon-feeding

plate to mouth, eye to eye, filling me up
with enriched and restorative affixion

uniting me to a fine feeling
all I had to do was wait

the wisdom was there, resting ahead
alluringly offering itself to me

permissive power

with all of her power

she keeps us inside
for the worst part of each year

we're drowning from the air
inside our abodes

we avoid serenity
run away to technology
and force ourselves to sleep

avoiding permission
to give ourselves a chance to be brave
and step down from doing

step into just being
she guides us inside
as she comes crashing down

we never see it as an invitation
to drink wine and whisky
and dive into a jewelled journal
to surrender to our inner world

we'll never discern our divine
'fore the drop in
how do we do it?
it's simple

be kind to yourself
you have one thing to worry about,
as you give yourself permission
for liberation

willingly be the voice
of the inexhaustible expression
of celestial's clouds
now, let's just play pretend for a moment

and call it that single and rare time of year
to build meaningful relationships with ourselves
and find that deeply satisfying connection with those we love

unfortunately, this impedes fear into so many of us
and we would do just about anything to avoid it
it encourages anesthetizing and drinking

numbing ourselves into a disorienting sleep
and smoking ourselves high
totally tripping, it comes with the season

for those of us who rest
encourage awareness to take place

in the end, we come out stronger
especially since she kept us in

with all of her power

falling in love

rain reminds me of when I was falling in love
driving through the mountains in the northern part of the sky
soaking wet in the middle of the misty night
escaping the potential planted painful rejection
proudly leaving and accelerating my way home

rain reminds me of when I woke up the next morning
it was emotionally disordering
unscripted and alluring
everything fell silent
phone dead, power out
and I realized

rain reminds me of when I saw his face again
I felt my heart bashfully jumping to skyward bliss
as the showers came down slashing
that perishing ostentatious sound
losing connection to all my senses
bewilderment of where I was
and I woke up drowning
in the sea of his fortuitous soul

rain reminds me of when I left
parting from all the invoked love
that we so sentimentally spawned
tears streaming down his face
cries dripping onto my heart
he read words of French love to me
while trickling emotional passion
as it fell as the crow flies to my soft sleeve

rain reminds me of when I was gone
growing ecstatically from all that time apart
giving me a chance to connect with created community
tying a string from the heart of my spirit
to the nature of my neighbours

rain reminds me of when I returned home
I had to step off the plane to realize it *was* home
you found me while carrying flowers with a sign
commitment through a single stone
genuinely considering me
as your home

droplets of false love

stepping into my car
already soaked
mind to toes
door to door

saying an ungraceful farewell
shy of nobly driving away
seeing him intentionally
watching me closely

tears falling down his face straight onto his sweater
matching the incredible gloom of this god-awful weather
my window becomes so dreadfully wet
from the terrible fall of this unthinkably, unhappy hope

I couldn't see anything past my eyes, anyways
drops of sea began rippling down me
harmonizing with the glistening beads
of the whole covers that reside in the ether of the sky

scared to leave the little coastal town
departing for the second almost-regrettable time
noticing unmitigated truth in my choice
following that inner voice, to relinquish

becoming charred like coal
never husked from the base of a winter's fire
I overstayed my welcome
and it was time to go and grow

my life was footsteps away from becoming a mess
I couldn't resist this disarray any longer
I needed to learn how to pick it all back up again
and devour the food for my soul

by promising myself
to never lie again about who I am
and it was all because I falsely convinced myself
I was in love

fall to inspire

watching the ways, she drops
from the clouds, and melts
into the earth, carving
a new beginning

what she comes with

she comes with the days we fall lost while flowing inward
those tender moments as we crave and live for long mornings
with that cozy autumn sweater wearing weather
delicious with hot coffee and thick cream
styled with a homemade pottery mug
and dusty dry cinnamon sticks

she comes with the times when we want to sit by the fire
with a Bordeaux styled glass of Syrah
uncurled from the vines of the Okanagan Valley
and a wool blanket to cover our freezing cold toes
reading a book that invites us to go
on a remarkably mystifying journey home

she comes with space for meaningful connection
through conversations that have been missed overtime
something new to be gleaned
wrongfully learned is let go
we're getting too old
to not really know

she comes with the moments we receive a new journal
ready to fill it
front page to back
bottom to top
with four blank folios always remaining

could this come with a kaleidoscopic glass of wine, too?

perfect,
three please
all for me

she's here

the rain hears us
watch
how she reacts
when she receives us

the rain listens to us
notice
what she does
when she responds to us

the rain talks to us
witness
the feeling
when she speaks to us

the rain serves us
please
begin to thank her
as she teaches us

responsibility

he's the architect
of romantic evenings

laying down
a plan of quixotic scenes

compelling the victims
to stay together

none can leave, as
it's all meant to be

rainstorm's decisions

once he gifted me a night right out of a fairy tale
to share evening and morning rituals with that man I loved
having no understanding of the ardour already taking over me
we connected as the sound of sheets slashed
creating clatter overhead the ceiling

as I pondered a decision to let my guard down
and share a bed and brush my teeth with this delicious man
I only stayed as it was so unsafe to make my way home
pretending it was entirely against my will
he handed me a new bamboo toothbrush
exclusively charming my heart toward his

he never kissed me
never cuddled me
never touched me
never brushed against my shoulder
never made a move
never lost my trust

he just lied next to me
pouring his love into me
from the other side of the bed

all because of this blessed rainfall
a special night outside of our regular trend

natural exchange

she's so soft, desirable
notice what she does
for you, for us, for me

and witness
she never asks
for anything back

don't scare it away

I wanna scream
turn off my hearing
shed away my listening

imagine a life without it
in a forever-lasting drought
the damage it would cause

can we all just agree
not to ask for that here
by screaming at the top of our lungs

let's open our ears
expand our listening
of the awareness of its' divinity

encouraging it to keep coming
we would never survive a drought, so
let's not allow the cessation

because we would all regret it
and hold remorse
for its permanence of leaving

clouds

filling itself up
assembling all it can
shy of the downpour

wiping us clear
of undesired energy
generating life
inventing mass

density forming the scene
for the delicious moment
our date arrives

begging

and then there are times
when it never arrives
my body collapses into craving
like an adolescent longs for sex

I look outside
every forty-four seconds, begging
the clouds to form
and air to become wet

years have gone by
waiting for so long,
it seems I'm desperate

to feel our oxygen air
drenched
in that delicious H-2-O,
but, it just won't fall

teasing us
the same way your date at prom teased you
under the table at dinner

space between

I look at the sky and I feel
everything around me is dry

my arms and eyes and feet
are beginning to flake

my hair is becoming crispy
like an uncooked French spaghetti

I look up with high hopes
of witnessing a drop of fresh marine

nothing makes its way down here
that hydrogen oxygen combination
completely halting itself to a stop

resting, at the borders between
the edges of the earth
and you and me

show up for me

I like when she's around
she gives me reason
to be slothful and idle
keeping me ceaselessly stirring
solely devoting to all that I yearn

I like when she's around
she keeps my mind off what's dirtying
my dinner dishes, drenching me
in her divine beauty
a cornucopia of fulfilled wishes

I like when she's around
she encourages me to unify
committing to faithfully falling
from the sky, to the ground,
interdependently

I like when she's around
she makes me feel free
by embodying complete ease
listening to the calls of no one
but her own pukka Being

I like when she's around
because, truthfully
it's the only time I feel
soulfully connected to me

beg to play

when I beg
it never comes
my heart begins
to slacken and slump

when I wait, patiently
it always arrives
a chance to notice that playing
of all the most sacred instruments

it's here, furthermore
it becomes clear
it's not she who is imparting this knowledge
her medium is what's teaching me

everything

as a pond
she's near-stillness
in subtle flow

as the sea
she's ever-changing
unrestrictedly

as a beverage
she's satiating
quenchingly serving

as the rain
she's everything
requesting patience

as a seer
she'll always be here
in those moments, that
we really need her

bow to gone beauty

even when she's gone
she's still here
by your side
in minuscule form

glistening
in the sunlight
splendour rippling
subtle sensations of the wind
nearby trees weaving
and waving
farewell

even when she's gone
we never forget
to bow down
to her beauty

wet lipstick

you know that moment
the one where your skin tingles?
let me explain.

the whole world loses every door, wall, and mountain
all becoming a flat plane
an ethereal breeze running along the earth's surface, rushing
around your toes, impressing a crisp canyon

your body becomes deliciously toasty
as you gulp the girdling gravity
and remember every moment

you know that moment?
right as your body feels like it's collapsing
but you never actually hit the ground falling
your legs are like over-cooked Italian spaghetti
the kind with almost too much sugar in the smooth tomato sauce
you manage to stay still enough
to keep the earth underneath your feet
because you don't wanna lose this moment

you know that moment?
your palms feel like they've been dipped in wet lipstick
and the feeling runs all the way up your pores
hot perspiration covers you from the inside out
taking slothy-like strides, submerging you in the moisture
the kind that you attentively yearn

you know that moment?
it feels like it just rained

and you breathe in the washed and virtuous air
it's like it's your first time breathing
maybe it is your first time breathing
in this way, anyway

you know that moment?
when your heart is racing so fast
it feels like one giant thump
thump
thump
thump

your whole body feels like it's releasing
surrendering to this thump
thump
thump
thump

you know that moment?
where the matching breath is hovering just over your nose
and you are being seen for the first time
you are being felt for the first time
you are being touched for the first time
in this way, anyway

you know that moment?
where grip is deliciously holding you like a snake
feeling like a hug from the world around you
one you find so goddamn yummy

you know that moment?
you realize you forgot to breath
so you take everything in, finally
swallowing sips of fine air, feeling

oxygen massage your mind
for the very first time

you know that moment?
where nerves start to shake you
as you enjoy this wet lipstick
and look into the eyes of the other
being held up with a gaze
seeing the reflection in his eyes
of your mustard-yellow and tiger-striped iris
shivers find themselves
on the surface of your whole body

you know that moment?
where you're somehow experiencing *everything*
your mouth is salivating
as you're impatiently waiting
and nothing has even happened yet

you know that moment?
your breathing is matching
in divine time with the other
and time is slowing
right
down

wait, has time stopped?
hmmm...
or are you only dreaming of wet lipstick?

you know that moment?
when you look at the clock,
and you realize this is why
your heart is taking such a loud and long thump

thump

thump

thump

because,

in all of this time

in all of these moments

only about four seconds have moved on by

as you've been drowning in wet lipstick

you know that moment?

where you could stand in this still time forever

because you don't ever want to leave

always pausing to stay

so, you do

you know that moment?

where you've nearly lost all physical sensation

your body feels like it's about to collapse

it's so covered in wet lipstick

that you could wring yourself out with a towel

you know that moment?

where it finally *almost* happens

and your body is being pushed up against a wall

your lips are softly brushed with the breath of the other

you're tickled with the soft eyelashes of the body just above you

you know that moment?

where it doesn't even feel like you're trying to do anything

you're just here

it's all just happening

so unbelievably and deliciously effortlessly

and you're repossessing blissful butterflies like a teenager again, but it feels like it's the first time

you know that moment?
you are connecting
through subtle, unwarranted movements of your body
intimacy giving your mind a chance to sweep clear
your heart gets to be loud and heard
and so easy to see

you know that moment?
you're finally being kissed
it feels like you've been waiting for this to come forever
but all it's been is simply this one,
single,
minuscule,
four second moment

all of this
is just one moment.
you know that moment?

I do,
take note
and listen carefully, because
I'll never actually share it with you.

worry free

the ocean never worries
when her next rain drop will fall

fall

stillness, eerie
breezelessness, lingering
trees, settling, into tranquillity
one last brush of the wind
picking all of it right up
pocketing into the sky
above us

and we
just
wait

five
four
three
two
one

now

pwooh-aaa-ooshhhh
forcefully falling hard to the earth
splattering to meet us all in one union
a peculiar subtle sense of distortion
as it knocks us from all angles
ooshhhh-aaa-whooop

gurgles from the ground
wind pulsing it side to side
falling on the top of our skulls

from toes
to crown
to nose
drenching us all
in this fine fresh fall

landing together

there are times it worries me
dropping dead

a quintessential invitation
into an unwanted forever

still and all
I'm wrong

I reminisce,
laugh and witness

since we all end up together
in the light of our shining treasure

here

dripping
light projecting
between the sheaths
of the clouds

dropping
night protecting
each and every tear
of the stars

release

in the middle of the night
sounds of substantial sadness
drop heavily above us, devouring
like a newborn breastfeeding

sky embodying
prominence of proclamation
the perfect paradigm
always awaiting atop

yet we never learn
which is so sad to know
because we have a teacher, always
speaking from right above us

instead, we're fighting
storing sadness
deep in our bodies
until we're about to burst

we have no other option
than to completely let go
and honour the agreement
our body has made to our soul

if only we could learn
the intangible vigour of release
the sky has always held
and taught, so accurately

flying

you're not the only one here
we all have graciously arrived

joining you in celebration, simply
because you've already landed

smooth as a pilot, flying
the experience of nearly a century

we're committed
to start this journey

we've actually already left
to go on this adventure with you

free

crashing and slashing on top of the leaves
bending them until they snap

the strong stand firm and tall
unabashedly planting themselves

never allowing what's below to get hurt
and so,

they are free of guilt
from a fatal fall

cozy

it starts falling
hop right back into bed

wish for it to drop harder
don't have to get up again

cozy up in his manly arms
lay in the soothing soft sheets

don't stop me from drowning
in all that I please

as there's nothing else
I would ask the rain to give me

sea

it's time

letting go
of where we are

un-remembering
of what we are

releasing expectations
of who we are

letting ourselves
just be, simply settling

into what we want to see
as our reality, delicately and deeply

the rain settles into the ocean
our bodies settle onto the Earth

they are not characterized rain drops, only
we are not individual bodies, only

we often believe that's all we are
but really, we're all just one great big and vast sea

freedom

shouting loudly
I have forgotten
about all that awful pain
and dreaded scarcity

only remembering generosity
and freedom free-falling
right onto me
sovereignty submerging me

wait
and stop time for a moment
can you smell that?
mmmhhhmmm

what a delicious taste
of enlightened brilliance

can you hear that?
could this be freedom?

it must be
because, if this isn't
I don't think I'm ready
to know what freedom really is

but, if this *is*
please accompany me
in each and every moment
until death liberates us more

be kind

time discontinues
as he enters the room
masking all that is happening

wrapping me in a wet blanket
generously gifted

a warm heart
to a kind soul

at least I'd hope
it's gifted to a kind soul

because that kind soul
is supposed to be me

finally

it's pouring, and
my heart's mirroring the actions
of the whole world, around me

rain is here
giving me time to relinquish
and release, completely

I have kept everything, bottled
inside for long
I just have to sulk

drop into deep rest
sit fruitlessly on my seat
lose sight of my breath for a moment

and then,
everything comes bursting
straight out of me

think of the way
it all falls from the sky
after our great Mother holds it entirely in

courageous retention
her absolute best
to stay thriving, sunny, and stunning

but, it's hard
pre-pwoooohishhhh,
we almost let it all go

it puddles
into a thick parachute above
the centre of the dense fog sack snaps
it all comes tumbling down

notice everyone below, eager
to experience the reverberation of release
grateful for it to finally pour over
after wishing for it for so long

pending trust

a confronting conversation
begins like a torrential rainfall
failing to hold it all together
bottling itself up
into and behind the clouds

in one small moment
everything drops
falls far down
below us
until the anger passes

pending...
it's all still here
even after everything was said
yelled, claimed, wished for
...pending

it's trying
to wash itself clean
doing more damage at first
but coming out fresh in the end
my favourite day, clean laundry day

a heavy rainfall
destroys us
before nourishing us
my sweet darling,
can't you see?

nature is a precise echo of humanity

what she does
how she holds back
how she lays down
how she starts over

how she embodies mastery
of great irrevocable change
how inspiring to see
revelling in our power to participate
in a revolution of exchange

how prevailing we are
even during the dreaded change
look, see, cease thinking, that
we are anything nature is not
because we are just like her

everything we believe
will be challenged
when we listen
very closely
to these wise words:

we are allowed to feel pain
and plunge
into the land of mistakes
creating unwanted chaos
in all areas around us

no worries, my friend
have good intention
everything will work out
before too long,
just remember

trust the power of your exchange
it will bring world-shattering change
to the way we all represent connection
uprising in authenticity
through uncomfortability

the result:
we unify
into one virtuous Being
alike the rain unifying
into the single mass
of the soil and the sea

never owing

laying in the heat of the sun
everything around me is soaked
I look straight out the gap in my ceiling
to see the perfectly shaded palm tree covering
protecting me from the rapid downpour
of that unwelcomed rain

long and green heavenly leaves
sun reflecting on it so generously
such an incredible gift of exchange
the sun feeds the tree with light
the tree feeds the sun with beauty

and no one ever dared
to ask for an exchange
and still, I watch them thriving
never owing or owning
and more importantly
always reciprocating

devour me

eat me up
nourish me, too

a heart I'll lose myself in
foundation so soft
of water and soot

pleasure of the Soul
a gift from the Earth

nothing is tainted
and nothing is missing
the rain devours the space

as I eat up his heart
and he devours me, too

naked

I'm slowly getting ready
to willingly offer my body to you

the moment just shy of the instance everything drops
and all my clothes fall right off my skin

I lay down and wait patiently
my heart starts beating enchantingly

a melody of heat comes from within
boiling drops of rain as they fall onto me

deeply refreshing every peeling pore
giving me erotic tingles and goosebumps

I'm being touched
for the first time

the rain has never done so much for me
it's always making sweet love to me

my body floats in the abyss of the mist
grateful to be giving it entirely to you

you're the only one I can offer it to
enrapturing the sight of it feeding us

octaves above

there's always a time when everything seems to settle again
after she's firmly laid herself on the ground
giving her body up

she's nourishing us gently and easily
we notice the surprising
ceased splashing

exactly when we believed
it may never end,
what a gift of love

through the remarkable sheets of rain
falling down unconditionally
from four octaves above

start to surrender

it all comes crashing down
angry at each part of us

lightening up
relieving us

of any grief, or tension
that has yet to ever leave us

let's please just allow it
or else it'll keep trying

until we finally surrender
and we cannot handle her regularity

over and over and over again
it'll drain us into nothing

just have her do her job
let the pain of the rain fleet from us all

notice and change

imagine the moment
you've finally opened your gift
you look right inside, to witness
complete inherent beauty

your heart starts to settle
as the moon of the evening lifts
up, just a little
into the love painted rainbow-striped sky

holding itself overhead
stars of freedom shooting
across outer space
in search of finding one another

now, imagine the moment
you take your eyes off your gift
you bashfully dip
into the creamy awareness of the abyss

rediscovering what's around you
and you witness
one simple thing, changing
your life forever

everything you just had the pleasure of seeing
a clear mirror of the world you're living
and here you are, appreciating the gift
yet, unable to appreciate your world

but, don't you worry sweet child
your world is entirely the same
and so, now that you know
this is your chance to finally change

home

raindrops land on the car's window
I sit in the street of my busy hometown, leaning
against the delicious dewy crystallized glass

softly watching each drop fall, swiftly
listening to prized poetic harmony
the spoken words of Bon Iver

music elevating sensations
body, mind, ears, and tears
deeply breathing

noticing the way each drop falls
effortlessly coming together
unswervingly uniting into the other's weather

dropping down in smooth collection
this single shared long breath
of the many shades and sheets
our rainfall's been crafting forever

find me

dark and short days
the end of November, running
from clear drops of aqua

something is wrong
I'm sprinting in the rain, earning
that unfortunately unfamiliar feeling

being myself completely
I stop and simply just stand
my body begins to melt and drown

all while I'm still softly breathing
my heart thumps, body receiving
each ounce pouring on top of me

I was trying to escape
this part of the world
until I realized

I am this world
I've found myself
as part of the rain

grey to colour without you

sitting at home, waiting for you
you promised you would return

counting dents below the roof
numbering cracks on the walls

doing my best not to check on you
making my waiting needy

staying present, with this inconsistent scheme
that rests above me on the ceiling

I look out the window to see you're arriving
the wind frolicking and clouds as grey as your heart

last time you forgot to show up for me
I had no hope for you, on this current day

I guess I had a little bit of fervent hope
nevertheless, I'm here waiting again

for your heart to turn into colour
even so, everything comes crashing down

leaving me with nothing, except lost presence
a sunset sky and a rainbow rise

to be honest, though, it'll do
it's actually far better than you

sedate me

put me to sleep,
won't you?

I can't bear the thought,
of getting up again

nourish me to dream

watch me doze off and away
as I listen to the sounds of love
you are dressing our shared space with

once I fall asleep
you keep me nourished, until
you get too loud and wake me up again

it's only you, I feel gratitude
for waking me up as I sleep deeply
discovering all my dreams

dreams I would have never known
and only did because of you
dressing our shared space with willful, intrinsic love

flo into my manifestation

my childhood shook my belief in romanticism
witnessing broken relationships and abandoned promises

my naive adolescence served me a nearly unreservedly lost faith in
intimacy
involving myself with wrong and abusive teen boys

my early twenties withheld me from indulgence in lasting
relationships
choosing boys based on, 'damn, you're cute'

instead of men from a place of, 'ouuu, I feel your heart.'
I encouraged an idiosyncratic resentment regarding romanticism

choosing unserving non-lasting relationships, nothing beyond
the occasional coffee in the morning and glass of wine in the
evening

that all can be great, but it doesn't warm my heart,
feed my body, or guide my soul

long ago I decided it was enough
refusing to base my heart's happiness on clichés

deciding to have moments of intimacy with men world-wide
withholding boundaries that may have served me at the time

placing myself nonchalantly, with these discombobulated folk
deeply shy of finding true beauty and trust in them

this boundaryless purpose was creating tender pain
I was getting attached to all the wrong men

not caring one little bit about the noble and virtuous others
heavily dropping me into a deeply empty well of unfulfilling love

last year I decided that was enough, too
as the rain dropped layers of wisdom

soaking me in monsoon season
it should've been expected

even the rain was telling me to let go of it all
and learn from it to start anew

the result was a handwritten letter to the universe
sharing my readiness for someone aligned and true

'I'm ready for real love, I will prove it the moment it drops in'
I said, sharing this with my best friend

he would often say to me,
'Jenn, you need to get laid!'

laughter would spiral
tears sometimes transpired

my heart stayed open
game for the approaching adventure

'I'm ready!' I kept saying
I thought that no one was hearing

but, I kept repeating
and it turned out my best friend was fortuitously listening

flo from friendship to love

your heart was listening and following
so long without comprehension
still in the midst of monsoon

your heart was the universe
I was sending my messages to
and neither of us had any damn idea

until one day
you finally heard it
and saw me like you never did before

you looked at me with new eyes
a ready heart
and an open Soul

so we dove
and we acted courageously
with love and sweat and tears

my message was being heard and my heart broke
tenderly open thanks to you, your heart,
and your all-so-familiar soul

thanks to us
our worlds finally started colliding
after so much time resisting

and today I stand by your side
I am completely and madly in love
with both, us and you

take a shower

so much animosity in this world
a place so capable of love,
what is everyone crying for?

tears are dropping in great quantities
disposing everything that's not plentiful
triumphing a worldwide thunderstorm

they're all still bawling uncontrollably
what is everyone *really* crying for?
please tell me because I am at a loss

let's wash ourselves off with a shower of love
oooouuu ahhhh, I laugh
only if it were that easy

agreement

they are suffering
in such overwhelming
and everlasting misery
the real and sad victims
of their very own actions
antagonists of the world

and it all comes crashing down
tears have dried up inside of them
the rain doing what it can to renourish them
helping them find the innate love that they really are
but they just aren't allowing themselves to feel it
not yet, anyway

they feel they're not enough
not supported enough
understood enough
loved enough

let's all just agree
to love them unconditionally
you may sign your contract where you wish
and how you wish
please, just do it today

join me

the rain gives me a moment to take a step back, zoom out, and
breathe deep
so I can start to look at myself and see all the growth I must create
I'm tired of being in a world that lacks sincere support for us all
we need a world where people believe in themselves
a world of complete integration and acceptance

we need a world of kindness and devotion
to ourselves and to you and each other
we need a world of divine self-love
a world of pure, marvelous love
we need a world of creation
I will create a world
of generous love.

are you in?

let go

I'm waiting for the next chapter to unfold
but, it's still pouring buckets of minuscule soft crystals

patterns too perfect for me, becoming harder
to resist the temptation of letting go
so, I do

a new beginning

it's because of the rain
that we know
we always have a fresh start
after one hard fall

your dream

when you watch me falling,
what is it that you're hoping for?

trust and thanks

I'm seated here, alone and wondering
if I could have done anything better
or more right, or even more wrong

my tendency, perhaps
was terribly ineloquent
I don't know what else I could have done

here, I close my eyes and rest next to her
and listen for her divine guidance
mmmm... receiving... mmmm

'you did your best with all you know and what you have,'
is what she's whispering to me
'oh, and, one more thing,' she remembers

she says:
you've got this
trust yourself

have faith in your mistakes
see all that you've become
and what you've brought together

trust who you are
all of your moment-plus-long symposiums
the people who grace you

believe in where you find yourself
with purpose
on Saturday mornings

trust everything
don't speculate anything
you have created your whole existence

in the same way, that
the sun and the stars and the earth
have taken that sincere time
to paint the dusk covered sky
you will never change what you have done

in the same way, that
the sun can't change the colors
he brushed along the surface of our mother
in those moments sandwiching our daylight sky
you will only ever grow into becoming

in the same way, that
the sky reaches a clear climax
one that perpetually prolongs
after a stormy day of growing pains
and into a clear night with endless stars

trust, please
and thank you
for coming on this date with me
I promise to always be here for you

love always,
Rain

CPSIA information can be obtained
at www.ICGtesting.com
Printed in the USA
BVHW031934070321
601957BV00008B/344